ARCTIC REGION

A unique ecosystem, the Arctic is located north of 66° latitude in an area called the Arctic Circle. It consists of a vast frozen ocean of drifting ice bordered by lands of treeless tundra. The permanent ice is 10-13 ft. (3-4 m) thick and covers about three million square miles (8,000,000 sq. km). The bedrock at the North Pole is 1400 ft. (330 m) below sea level. The area stays below freezing for over half of the year and is battered by strong winds that can cause temperatures to plummet as low as -94°F (-67.8°C).

Despite the inhospitable nature of the climate, the Arctic supports large populations of species that have adapted to the environment and thrive here. It remains one of the few areas on Earth where many species live free, with lives devoid of human contact.

The tundra is covered with vegetation including dwarf shrubs, grasses, mosses, sedges and lichens. These plants provide food and cover for a variety of small animals including lemmings, voles and hares which are a critical food source for larger mammals including the Arctic fox. Large mammals unique to the Arctic include the polar bear, musk ox, walrus, caribou (reindeer), bowhead whale and bearded seal.

The Arctic tundra is a vast, treeless plain.

Waterford Press publishes reference guides that introduce readers to nature observation, outdoor recreation and survival skills. Product information is featured on the website: www.waterfordpress.com

978-1-58355-829-4 $7.95 U.S. $9.95 CAN

Text & illustrations © 2013, 2023 Waterford Press Inc. All rights reserved. Photos © iStock Photo. To order or for information on custom published products please call 800-434-2555 or email:orderdesk@waterfordpress.com.

For permissions or to share comments email:editor@waterfordpress.com. 2306806

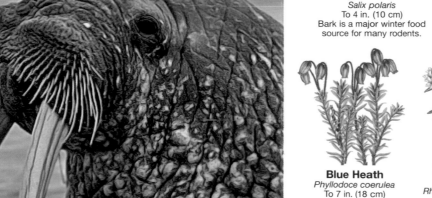

ARCTIC WILDLIFE

A Folding Pocket Guide to Familiar Animals & Plants of the Arctic & Subarctic Regions

T0124005

TUNDRA PLANTS

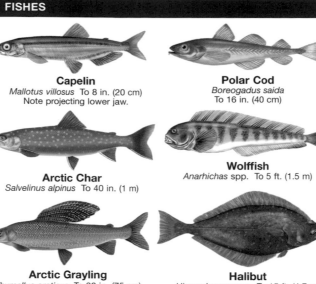

Arctic Cotton Grass
Eriophorum scheuchzeri
To 12 in. (30 cm)

Bog Laurel
Kalmia spp.
To 8 in. (20 cm)
Evergreen shrub has leathery leaves.

Scurvy-grass
Cochlearia spp.
To 8 in. (20 cm)
Sailors used to eat this plant which is a good source of vitamin C.

Arctic Willow
Salix polaris
To 4 in. (10 cm)
Bark is a major winter food source for many rodents.

Snow Buttercup
Ranunculus nivalis
To 10 in. (25 cm)

Bog Blueberry
Vaccinium uliginosum
To 2 ft. (60 cm)
Bell-shaped, pinkish flowers bloom in June and are succeeded by blue berries in summer.

Blue Heath
Phyllodoce coerulea
To 7 in. (18 cm)

Narrow-leaved Labrador Tea
Rhododendron palustre
To 40 in. (1 m)

Arctic Poppy
Papaver radicatum
To 2 ft. (60 cm)
The most northern growing plant in the world is found above latitudes of 83°.

Reindeer Lichen
Cladonia rangiferina
To 4 in. (10 cm)

Sphagnum Moss
Sphagnum spp.
To 8 in. (20 cm)
Tassel-like plant heads are greenish to red in color. Forms peat bogs over time.

Purple Saxifrage
Saxifraga oppositifolia
To 2 in. (5 cm)
Mat-forming plant has scale-like leaves.

Crowberry
Empetrum nigrum
To 6 in. (15 cm)
Heather-like shrub has black, juicy berries.

FISHES

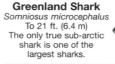

Capelin
Mallotus villosus To 8 in. (20 cm)
Note projecting lower jaw.

Polar Cod
Boreogadus saida
To 16 in. (40 cm)

Arctic Char
Salvelinus alpinus To 40 in. (1 m)

Wolffish
Anarhichas spp. To 5 ft. (1.5 m)

Arctic Grayling
Thymallus arcticus To 30 in. (75 cm)
Large dorsal fin is distinctive.

Halibut
Hippoglossus spp. To 15 ft. (4.7 m)
Huge flat fish weighs up to 710 lbs. (320 kg).

Greenland Shark
Somniosus microcephalus
To 21 ft. (6.4 m)
The only true sub-arctic shark is one of the largest sharks.

LAND MAMMALS

Collared Lemming
Dicrostonyx spp.
To 5 in. (13 cm)

Arctic Ground Squirrel
Urocitellus parryii
To 15 in. (38 cm)

Tundra Shrew
Sorex tundrensis
To 6 in. (15 cm)
Note pointed nose.

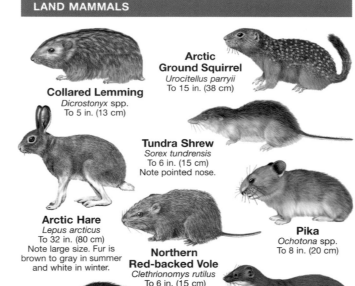

Arctic Hare
Lepus arcticus
To 32 in. (80 cm)
Note large size. Fur is brown to gray in summer and white in winter.

Northern Red-backed Vole
Clethrionomys rutilus
To 6 in. (15 cm)

Pika
Ochotona spp.
To 8 in. (20 cm)

Wolverine
Gulo gulo To 44 in. (1.1 m)

Short-tailed Weasel
Mustela erminea To 14 in. (35 cm)
Note white feet. Coat may turn white in winter. Also known as ermine or stoat.

LAND MAMMALS

Arctic Wolf
Canis lupus arctos To 6.5 ft. (2 m)
Lives at latitudes north of 70°.

Arctic Fox
Alopex lagopus To 3 ft. (90 cm)

Muskox
Ovibos moschatus
To 8 ft. (2.4 m)

Caribou (Reindeer)
Rangifer tarandus To 8 ft. (2.4 m)

MARINE MAMMALS

Pacific Walrus
Odobenus rosmarus
To 12 ft. (3.6 m)

Polar Bear
Ursus maritimus
To 11 ft. (3.3 m)
Spends most of its life on shifting sea ice and is considered a marine mammal.

Bearded Seal
Erignathus barbatus
To 9 ft. (2.7 m)
Named for its abundant whiskers.

Harp Seal
Pagophilus groenlandicus
To 6 ft. (1.8 m)
Has a black mark on its back. Young pups are yellow-white.

Hooded Seal
Cystophora cristata To 8.5 ft. (2.6 m)
Male has an inflatable bladder on its head.

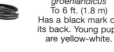

Ringed Seal
Phoca hispida
To 6 ft. (1.8 m)
Has silver rings on back and sides. The most common Arctic seal.

MARINE MAMMALS

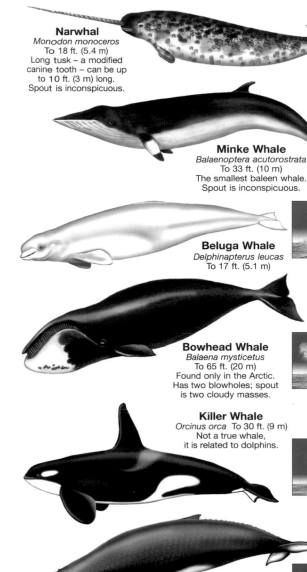
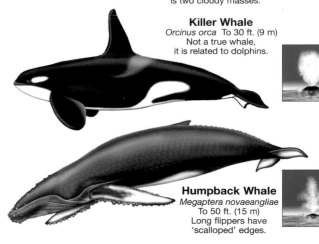

Narwhal
Monodon monoceros
To 18 ft. (5.4 m)
Long tusk – a modified canine tooth – can be up to 10 ft. (3 m) long. Spout is inconspicuous.

Minke Whale
Balaenoptera acutorostrata
To 33 ft. (10 m)
The smallest baleen whale. Spout is inconspicuous.

Beluga Whale
Delphinapterus leucas
To 17 ft. (5.1 m)

Bowhead Whale
Balaena mysticetus
To 65 ft. (20 m)
Found only in the Arctic. Has two blowholes; spout is two cloudy masses.

Killer Whale
Orcinus orca To 30 ft. (9 m)
Not a true whale, it is related to dolphins.

Humpback Whale
Megaptera novaeangliae
To 50 ft. (15 m)
Long flippers have 'scalloped' edges.

Finback Whale
Balaenoptera physalus
To 80 ft. (24 m)

The majority of Arctic birds are non-residents that migrate here every year during breeding season when food is abundant.

Red-throated Loon
Gavia stellata
To 25 in. (63 cm)

Pacific Loon
Gavia pacifica To 25 in. (63 cm)

Yellow-billed Loon
Gavia adamsii
To 38 in. (95 cm)

Arctic Loon
Gavia arctica To 27 in. (68 cm)
White neck stripes are more obvious than those on Pacific Loon.

Canada Goose
Branta canadensis
To 45 in. (1.14 m)

Brant
Branta bernicla
To 2 ft. (60 cm)
Note white neck mark.

Barnacle Goose
Branta leucopsis
To 28 in. (70 cm)

Greater White-fronted Goose
Anser albifrons
To 30 in. (75 cm)
Note white ring at bill base.

Tundra Bean Goose
Anser serrirostris
To 33 in. (83 cm)
Breeds on the Russian tundra.

Snow Goose
Chen caerulescens
To 31 in. (78 cm)

Horned Puffin
Fratercula corniculata
To 14 in. (35 cm)

Atlantic Puffin
Fratercula arctica
To 12 in. (30 cm)

Tufted Puffin
Fratercula cirrhata
To 16 in. (40 cm)

Razorbill
Alca torda
To 18 in. (45 cm)

Common Murre
Uria aalge
To 17 in. (43 cm)

Thick-billed Murre
Uria lomvia
To 19 in. (48 cm)
Note white mark on bill.

Dovekie
Alle alle To 9 in. (23 cm)

Parakeet Auklet
Aethia psittacula
To 10 in. (25 cm)
Note stubby red bill.

Black Guillemot
Cepphus grylle
To 14 in. (35 cm)

Pelagic Cormorant
Phalacrocorax pelagicus
To 30 in. (75 cm)
Note red throat and face.

King Eider
Somateria spectabilis
To 2 ft. (60 cm)

Long-tailed Duck
Clangula hyemalis
To 22 in. (55 cm)

Common Eider
Somateria mollissima
To 28 in. (70 cm)

Steller's Eider
Polysticta stelleri
To 18 in. (45 cm)

Spectacled Eider
Somateria fischeri
To 22 in. (55 cm)

Green-winged Teal
Anas crecca To 16 in. (40 cm)

Red-breasted Merganser
Mergus serrator To 27 in. (68 cm)
Note prominent head crest.

Surf Scoter
Melanitta perspicillata
To 20 in. (50 cm)

Harlequin Duck
Histrionicus histrionicus
To 17 in. (43 cm)

Northern Pintail
Anas acuta To 30 in. (75 cm)

Iceland Gull
Larus glaucoides
To 22 in. (55 cm)

Ivory Gull
Pagophila eburnea
To 17 in. (43 cm)

Black-legged Kittiwake
Rissa tridactyla
To 18 in. (45 cm)
Legs and wing tips are black.

Sabine's Gull
Xema sabini
To 14 in. (35 cm)
Black-bill is yellow-tipped.

Ross's Gull
Rhodostethia rosea
To 11 in. (28 cm)
Note small size.

Glaucous Gull
Larus hyperboreus
To 27 in. (68 cm)
Note large size.

Northern Gannet
Morus bassanus
To 40 in. (1 m)
Large white sea bird has black wing tips.

Arctic Tern
Sterna paradisaea
To 15 in. (38 cm)
Breeds in the Arctic and winters in the Antarctic. Migrates over 44,000 miles (70,000 km) each year, the longest migration of any animal on earth.

Long-tailed Jaeger
Stercorarius longicaudus
To 2 ft. (60 cm)
Much of its length is attributed to its long tail streamers.

Parasitic Jaeger
Stercorarius parasiticus
To 18 in. (45 cm)
Often seen harrassing terns and gulls.

Great Skua
Stercorarius skua
To 2 ft. (60 cm)
Dark seabird has white wing patches.

Pomarine Skua
Stercorarius pomarinus
To 26 in. (65 cm)
Note large size, yellowish neck and elongated tail streamer.

Manx Shearwater
Puffinus puffinus
To 10 in. (25 cm)

Leach's Storm-Petrel
Oceanodroma leucorhoa
To 8 in. (20 cm)
Note white rump and light bars on upperwings.

Northern Fulmar
Fulmarus glacialis To 18 in. (45 cm)
Ocean glider has a stubby yellow bill with tubelike nostrils.

American Golden-Plover
Pluvialis dominica
To 12 in. (30 cm)
Mantle is gold-spotted.

Semipalmated Plover
Charadrius semipalmatus
To 8 in. (20 cm)
Note single breast band.

Black-bellied Plover
Pluvialis squatarola
To 14 in. (35 cm)

Ruddy Turnstone
Arenaria interpres
To 10 in. (25 cm)

Purple Sandpiper
Calidris maritima
To 9 in. (23 cm)

Snipe
Gallinago gallinago
To 12 in. (30 cm)

Red Phalarope
Phalaropus fulicarius
To 8.5 in. (21 cm)

Red Knot
Calidris canutus
To 12 in. (30 cm)
Plump, red-breasted shorebird.

Red-necked Phalarope
Phalaropus lobatus
To 8 in. (20 cm)
Female is larger and more colorful than the male.

Dunlin
Calidris alpina
To 9 in. (23 cm)
Note black belly patch.

Whimbrel
Numenius phaeopus
To 20 in. (50 cm)
Note striped crown.

Baird's Sandpiper
Calidris bairdii
To 7.5 in. (19 cm)

Pectoral Sandpiper
Calidris melanotos
To 9 in. (23 cm)
Breast is heavily streaked.

Sandhill Crane
Antigone canadensis
To 4 ft. (1.2 m)

Long-billed Dowitcher
Limnodromus scolopaceus
To 12 in. (30 cm)

White-rumped Sandpiper
Calidris fuscicollis
To 8 in. (20 cm)
White rump is visible in flight.

Sanderling
Calidris alba
To 8 in. (20 cm)
Runs in and out with waves along shorelines.

Gyrfalcon
Falco rusticolus
To 25 in. (63 cm)

Snowy Owl
Bubo scandiacus
To 27 in. (68 cm)

White-tailed Sea Eagle
Haliaeetus albicilla
To 38 in. (95 cm)
Close cousin of the bald eagle is also called erne.

Peregrine Falcon
Falco peregrinus
To 20 in. (50 cm)

Rough-legged Hawk
Buteo lagopus
To 2 ft. (60 cm)
Note dark banded white tail and dark 'wrists.'

Common Raven
Corvus corax
To 27 in. (68 cm)
Call is a hoarse croak.

Rock Ptarmigan
Lagopus mutus
To 14 in. (35 cm)

Willow Ptarmigan
Lagopus lagopus
To 17 in. (43 cm)

Northern Wheatear
Oenanthe oenanthe
To 6 in. (15 cm)

Arctic Redpoll
Acanthis hornemanni
To 5 in. (13 cm)

Common Redpoll
Acanthis flammea
To 5 in. (13 cm)

Snow Bunting
Plectrophenax nivalis
To 8 in. (20 cm)

Lapland Longspur
Calcarius lapponicus
To 7 in. (18 cm)

Arctic Warbler
Phylloscopus borealis
To 5 in. (13 cm)
Note prominent 'eyebrow.'

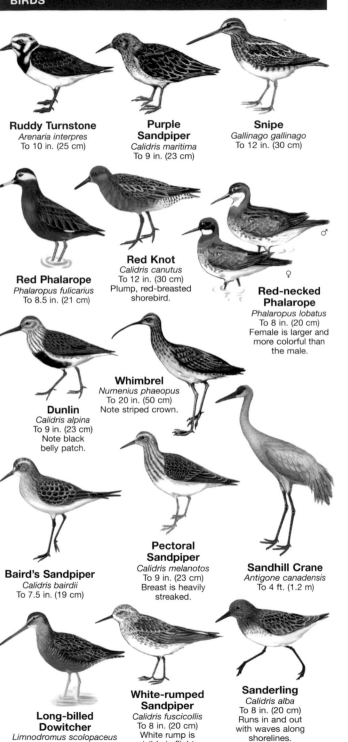